Finding God in the Hunger Games

30 Devotions to Inspire Faith

Selena Sarns
(with Heather Nordeman)

the
BiblePeople.com

Finding God in the Hunger Games

© 2013 TheBiblePeople.com

Published by TheBiblePeople.com. Our mission is to encourage people to read, understand, and apply the Bible.

Printed in the United States of America.

Contents

Reading 1
We All Need a Savior

Romans 3:23 (ESV) *"For all have sinned and fall short of the glory of God."*

THE PEOPLE OF Panem have utterly forsaken God. At no point in the *Hunger Games* trilogy does any character mention God, the Church, or even the afterlife—which is odd, considering the prevalence of death throughout the series. Yet in the evil and horror that characterizes the dystopian nation of Panem, Collins paints a vivid picture of sin taken to the greatest extremes. The rich oppress the poor; absolute power and wealth belong to a malevolent few; starvation, homelessness, fear, and disease abound. In the opening chapters of *The Hunger Games*, we learn that the nation of Panem has become a paragon of sin through human error: failing in our stewardship of the earth, the planet suffered major devastation, followed by years of war and human strife. By pushing the evidence of human sin to such extremes, Collins presents a world in which we cannot ignore the certainty that human beings have rebelled against God.

To fully demonstrate sin's hold over Panem, Collins

makes the central action of the trilogy a game so repulsive and evil that we must confront the horrific depths of human sin. Child sacrifice, child soldiers, and children murdering other children are among the most evil concepts we can imagine; and these are the very driving forces behind the imagined Hunger Games. The very concept of the "sacrifice" of child "tributes" is a perverted twist on the idea that, after the Fall, God required sacrifices to atone for human sin.

In this alternate reality, we can readily accept the need for a savior. Suffering, division, oppression, fear, and slavery—these are the very things that plague us when we are subject to sin. Indeed, like the people of Panem, we need someone to save us from our bondage.

Suffering, division, oppression, fear, and slavery—these are the very things that plague us when we are subject to sin. Indeed, like the people of Panem, we need someone to save us from our bondage.

Reading 2
God Chooses Unlikely Heroes

I Corinthians 1:27 (ESV) *"God chose what is foolish in the world to shame the wise; God chose what is weak in the world to shame the strong."*

AT FIRST GLANCE, Katniss Everdeen is a very ordinary girl from District 12. Like many other children across Panem, her days are spent fighting to survive in an inhospitable environment. The daughter of a deceased coal miner, she is like countless other District 12 children who have lost their fathers to mining accidents and who worry about the welfare of their remaining family members. And, along with everyone in Panem's twelve districts, she wakes up on the morning of the reaping filled with terror.

Moreover, Katniss is a deeply flawed character: in the first chapter of *The Hunger Games*, she confesses that she taught herself to wear "an indifferent mask so that no one could ever read [her] thoughts." She trusts very few people and struggles to develop relationships even with those who genuinely care about her, including Gale, Peeta, her mother, and Prim. At different times, she uses both Gale and Peeta for her own selfish purposes, especially when she thinks they can help her survive. Throughout *Mockingjay*, Katniss herself continually struggles with her role as a rebel leader because she knows her flaws run so deep. She frequently acknowledges her limitations as the Mockingjay and wonders how she will be able to faithfully serve as the "face of the rebellion." And, of course, she is continually plagued by the knowledge that she is responsible for so many deaths, both in the Games and the subsequent war...

Like Katniss, the prophet Jeremiah was in his youth when he was summoned to be a voice to God's people; and the deeply flawed King David was a surprising choice for the King of Israel. Rahab, whose name appears in the lineage of Jesus, was a prostitute, and Mary was a "lowly handmaid." Even though Katniss is often selfish, stubborn, and unfeeling, those around her sense that she is capable of great things, and they know she will be a help to their cause. God often chooses very unlikely people to be the servants of his will. He knows what each of us is capable of, and he calls us to be heroes in our own small ways.

God often chooses very unlikely people to be the servants of his will. He knows what each of us is capable of, and he calls us to be heroes in our own small ways.

Reading 3
In Christ, We Are Set Free

Galatians 5:1 (ESV) *"For freedom Christ has set us free."*

THE CITIZENS IN the districts are held captive by the authorities in the Capitol, and especially by the Hunger Games. As it is mandatory for each district to send tributes, and as all of Panem's citizens are required to watch, the Games overshadow their existence with terror and perpetual threat. Katniss notes during the first reaping that the Hunger Games were devised in order to continually remind the citizens of Panem that they are completely at the mercy of the Capitol, and that if they step out of line, they could be destroyed in an instant. She describes the victory tour as, "the Capitol's way of keeping the horror fresh and immediate"—in other words, keeping the people enslaved to fear. In *Mockingjay*, the rebels who move to District 13 find that they are enslaved in new ways: forced underground, subjected to strict schedules and food rationings, and governed by a dictatorial leader. The very idea of "bread and circuses," as explained by Plutarch Heavensbee, recalls ancient tactics employed by Roman emperors to keep the populace from gaining too much power.

Katniss herself feels particularly stifled by the oppressive authorities that govern Panem and District 13. When she can, she escapes into the woods where she feels most free; when she cannot, Katniss feels suffocated. Yet in volunteering for Prim, and later agreeing to be the Mockingjay, Katniss willingly enters into a different kind of bondage. From the moment she becomes a tribute, she frequently refers to herself as a "pawn in their games"—meaning that she has surrendered all control of her own fate. When she becomes the Mockingjay, she loses even more power over her life. As the face of the rebellion, she can never be just herself, but she must be what the rebels need her to be in order to bring peace to Panem. And by fighting alongside the rest of her nation, Katniss does further the rebel cause and make possible Panem's deliverance from the oppressive rule of the Capitol.

Christ, too, sacrificed his will in order to restore peace on earth. Unlike the wills to which Katniss becomes subject, Christ surrendered himself to God's perfect, holy, loving will. It was necessary for God to enter into our experience in order to free us from our bondage to death. Through his Incarnation, Christ became subject to our humanity; he set aside his heavenly freedom in order to free us from our sin. In humbling himself to death on the cross, Christ made possible our deliverance from death to life eternal. And in doing so, he set the example of how we ought to live: entering into the Christian life, we are called to lay aside our will in order to find the true freedom that comes from living in God's will.

He set the example of how we ought to live: entering into the Christian life, we are called to lay aside our will in order to find the true freedom that comes from living in God's will.

Reading 4
Only Christ's Sacrifice Can Atone for Sins

1 John 2:2 (NIV) *"he is the atoning sacrifice for our sins."*

THE LAW OF Panem requires children to be sacrificed in payment for the "treachery" of previous generations. After the districts rebelled, the Capitol instituted the Treaty of Treason as a set of rules to ensure peace; it also established the tradition of the Hunger Games. "Tributes"—children selected to represent their district at the brutal and deadly Hunger Games—are sent to the Capitol as punishment for the rebellion during the Dark Days. All of Panem is subject to these laws, but they affect the poorest and most vulnerable people the most.

The very word "tribute," which Katniss notes is "synonymous with the word *corpse*," means payment or sacrifice. Therefore, when Katniss hears Prim's name called at the reaping, she knows her young and vulnerable sister has no hope of returning to District 12. Katniss's brave decision to volunteer in place of Prim saves her sister from certain death in the arena.

Katniss accepts the likelihood of her own death, because she would rather die in the Games than let her sister be killed. In this way, Katniss steps in as a sacrifice *in place of* her sister.

While we can applaud Katniss's courageous and sacrificial act—for it certainly saves her sister's life—we can also rejoice that God does so much more for us. When we had fallen into death and sin through our own fault, God sent his son, Jesus Christ, to be a sacrifice in our place. In the Old Testament, God gave the Law, which required pure and spotless lambs to be sacrificed in atonement for sin; but in dying on the cross for all the sins of humanity, Jesus freed us from this law by taking the weight of all our sin on himself. Since Christ willingly died for us and freed us from these laws, we are able to be "at one" with God. This is known in Christian theology as "atonement," which means "at-one-ment."

Katniss's bravery echoes Christ's words to his followers: "No one has greater love than this, to lay down one's life for one's friends," and in stepping in for her sister, Katniss certainly becomes a paragon of sacrificial virtue. In the end, though, only Christ can atone for our sins.

In the Old Testament, God gave the Law, which required pure and spotless lambs to be sacrificed in atonement for sin; but in dying on the cross for all the sins of humanity, Jesus freed us from this law by taking the weight of all our sin on himself.

Reading 5
There is Nothing Greater Than Unconditional Love

Isaiah 54:10 (NRSV) *"For the mountains may depart and the hills be removed, but my steadfast love shall not depart from you."*

IN MANY WAYS, Peeta Mellark is a paradigm of unchanging and steadfast love. During the first Hunger Games, he tells Katniss in the cave that he has loved her since he was five years old, and that even when he looked at other girls, he always thought of Katniss. And throughout the trilogy, Peeta never wavers in his love for her, despite her lukewarm affection toward him. He never asks Katniss to "reply in kind, to make any declaration of love," and yet he is completely unreserved about his love for her. He continually puts himself at risk to protect Katniss. As children, he risks a beating from his mother by giving the starving Katniss a piece of burned bread, and throughout the Hunger Games he clearly places his life in danger to preserve Katniss over and over again. Even when he is hijacked by the Capitol and turned against Katniss for a time, his love remains true underneath, and eventually he recovers himself and rediscovers anew his love for her.

Haymitch tells Katniss in *Catching Fire*, "You could live a hundred lifetimes and you still wouldn't deserve him." Indeed, her devotion to Peeta lacks the same steadfast surety that Peeta shows toward her. When Peeta first declares his love for Katniss at the 74th Hunger Games interview, she believes he is motivated by self-preservation; she distrusts Peeta despite his clear and unwavering love for her. Throughout *The Hunger Games* and much of *Catching Fire,* Katniss uses Peeta to survive the arena and threats from the Capitol. Only when they are sent back to the arena does Katniss begin to show that she is capable of returning the same feelings toward Peeta, and yet even toward the end of *Mockingjay*, Gale points out that Katniss only truly loves those who help her to survive—an alarming indictment of her character. Further, Katniss finds herself torn between her love for Peeta and her love for Gale. She is unable to commit wholeheartedly to either of these two men because her love changes in every circumstance.

Through Peeta, we see an example of how we ought to love. Yet, more often than not, we are like Katniss in our love for God and others. When we think we don't need God's love to survive, we forget to devote ourselves to him. Our love is dependent, conditional, and fickle. God's love is pure and steadfast. In Romans 8, Paul writes, "I am convinced that neither death, nor life, nor angels, nor rulers, nor things present, nor things to come, nor powers, nor height, nor depth, nor anything else in all creation, will be able to separate us from the love of God in Christ Jesus our Lord." We can rejoice that God's love will never depart from us, and we must strive to live our lives in steadfast love for God and our neighbor.

Our love is dependent, conditional, and fickle. God's love is pure and steadfast.

Reading 6
We Need Christ and Each Other

I John 4:11 (NRSV) *"Beloved, since God loved us so much, we also ought to love one another."*

ONE OF THE reasons Katniss distrusts people is because she has been let down so often in her life that she finds it difficult to have faith in others. For this reason, Peeta's declaration of love throws Katniss's world into confusion, and one of her greatest struggles throughout the trilogy is learning to rely on others as well as herself. Peeta and Katniss are completely dependent upon one another; since they must convince the world of their love in order to stay alive, these two characters are essential for one another's survival. In the dystopian nation of Panem, an alternate reality in which God makes no appearance, these two characters often find that they have only one another. They must be each other's advocate at all times.

The apostle Paul wrote, "Bear one another's burdens, and in this way you will fulfill the law of Christ." We are called as Christians to rely upon one another when we face too many burdens to carry by ourselves. When we are weakened by life's trials, we can find new strength in our relationships with each other. Learning to trust one another can be difficult, but as the Bible so often reminds us, Christian love is bound by duty to one another. We must both help others who are hurting and allow others to help us when we hurt. As Katniss and Peeta learn to rely upon each other, they grow to embody more and more the virtues of humility— the self-lowering that enables Christian love to grow strong and flourish.

At the same time, because Katniss and Peeta have only one another, their reliance upon each other is absolute. How terrifying to place all hope solely in the love and support of another human being! People are changing, fickle, and unreliable; in the Hunger Games trilogy Katniss regularly fails to love Peeta as she ought to love, and when Peeta is hijacked, even his love for Katniss becomes unstable. Christians are called to love one another because God loves us, and the outpouring of God's love is so great that we must share that love with others. Yet we also love one another with the knowledge that human beings are fallen and will disappoint us from time to time. God, however, is perfect and never fails in his love for us. We can rejoice that, while we must depend upon one another for support through life's trials, we also have the great hope of an Advocate in heaven who loves us and supports us at all times and in all circumstances. Our greatest calling in this life is to humble ourselves before others; in this way, we begin to see the world as God sees it.

We can rejoice that, while we must depend upon one another for support through life's trials, we also have the great hope of an Advocate in heaven who loves us and supports us at all times and in all circumstances

Reading 7
God Never Abandons the Poor, Afflicted, or Oppressed

1 John 3:17 (ESV) *"But if anyone has the world's goods and sees his brother in need, yet closes his heart against him, how does God's love abide in him?"*

KATNISS EVERDEEN'S NATURAL instinct is to protect the weak and those who suffer. The story begins with her heroic decision to protect her vulnerable and innocent sister from torture and death in the arena. As the story unfolds, however, Katniss realizes her responsibility to seek justice for all in Panem who are oppressed and persecuted by various authority figures. She particularly becomes a voice for the voiceless. As the "face of the rebellion," Katniss's prominence in the media allows her to speak for those who are suffering; she uses her notoriety both to stand up to the Capitol and to inspire hope for the rebels.

One of the turning points that enables Katniss to realize her bigger purpose occurs in *Mockingjay*, during a visit to a rebel hospital just before it is bombed. When she greets those who have been wounded fighting against the Capitol, she realizes that she means something very important to those who are suffering in the districts. These are victims of Snow's ruthless regime and power-hungry methods of political oppression. As she speaks to the wounded, she realizes that she herself has a power that she hitherto had not understood: the power to inspire others to hope that justice may one day come to Panem.

When Katniss helplessly watches Capitol bombers obliterate the hospital, she channels her outrage into a moving speech that is filmed and later aired across Panem. She points to the smoking ruins of the hospital and speaks for the "unarmed men, women, and children" who have been killed moments before. She implicates the Capitol, and then she calls Panem to action, saying, "We must fight back!"

As Christians, we are also called to fight back against those who oppress the poor, afflicted, and oppressed. God tells us to seek justice and love mercy, yet so often we try to ignore our responsibility to those who are in need. We have a duty to protect those who are weak and to speak up for those who are unable to speak for themselves. Christ frequently told his followers that when we help one another, we are participating in God's perfect love. If we, as Christians called by God to seek justice, do not speak up for those who cannot speak for themselves, who will?

As Christians, we are also called to fight back against those who oppress the poor, afflicted, and oppressed.

Reading 8
We Can Always Trust in God

Proverbs 3:5 (NRSV) *"Trust in the Lord with all your heart, and do not rely on your own insight."*

WHEN PEETA IS rescued from the Capitol in *Mockingjay,* he is not in control of his own mind and must place all of his trust upon the word of others to reconstruct what is true. He has been hijacked and cannot even rely on his own memories, as they have been altered by torture and mind-controlling techniques. Peeta, who has proven a trusting and good-natured character to this point, is disoriented by his inability to distinguish between illusion and reality. Since Katniss figures so prominently in these altered memories, his confusion is exacerbated by her previous ambiguity toward their relationship.

During the "Star Squad" mission to the Capitol, Peeta confesses his difficulty in distinguishing between truth and fiction; he then asks, "Who can I trust?" to which his squad replies that Peeta can trust them. The team devises a game called *Real or Not Real* in which Peeta can ask if something is true or false, and the team will help him discern between illusion and reality. During this mission, Peeta must place his trust completely in the hands of others. Of course, all the squad members rely upon each other for survival, but Peeta especially has to place extra faith in his fellows—he not only has his life at stake, but his whole identity as well. Peeta's willingness to place his trust completely in the hands of others, even when it is impossible to know for certain what their intentions may be, demonstrates his genuine good nature and openness to blindly trust in the will of others.

In the same way, Christians are sometimes called to place "blind trust" in God. We cannot know all of God's will for us, and sometimes his ways are inscrutable. Yet when we lean on our own understanding, we can lose sight of God's plan for us. By trusting everything we are to God's great love, we ensure that our lives are safely guided by the One who knows what is most real, true, and right for our lives. Only by placing our trust in God can we experience the certainty that truth is on our side.

By trusting everything we are to God's great love, we ensure that our lives are safely guided by the One who knows what is most real, true, and right for our lives

Reading 9
We Are Ignited by the Holy Spirit

Luke 4:18 (NRSV) *"The Spirit of the Lord is upon me, because he has anointed me."*

Katniss's stylist Cinna chooses to brand her as the "girl on fire." In the first Hunger Games, he literally lights her opening ceremonies costume on fire, and again for her interview with Caesar Flickerman, Cinna's dress ignites when she twirls the skirt. Not only does Cinna create a compelling image for Katniss that may help her win some sponsors, but he also ignites within her a spark of courage—during the opening ceremonies parade, she thinks to herself for the first time since the reaping that she may have a chance of surviving the Games. In *Catching Fire*, President Snow tells Katniss that Cinna's choice was prophetic. During a visit to her home, he threatens her and tells her, "You have provided a spark that, left unattended, may grow into an inferno…" In the events leading to the Quarter Quell, Cinna again designs a fire-themed wardrobe; this time, he designs costumes inspired by smoldering coal embers. And in *Mockingjay*, Katniss declares to the Capitol: "Fire is catching!"—a warning to those in power that the flame of justice is spreading across Panem. Collins clearly employs the fire motif with great intention: the trilogy is rife with images of fire, smoke, sparks, and flames. Further, Katniss's media presence as "the girl on fire" plays a central role throughout the novels.

When Cinna lights Katniss's dress on fire for the opening ceremonies of the 74th Hunger Games, he ignites in her a spark of courage that she carries throughout the remainder of the series. As she faces imminent death, Cinna bestows upon Katniss a gift more precious than anything else: hope. To realize that she has reason to hope, Katniss must first literally walk through fire. Ignited by the flames of her costume, she is anointed into her role as "the girl on fire." Through Cinna's creations, she becomes something greater than she imagined possible: a symbol of hope to an oppressed people. When she doubts herself, or when she feels she cannot continue in her task, Katniss merely has to remember that she is "Katniss Everdeen: The Girl on Fire," and she knows that she has been chosen for a great purpose and that she has been commissioned by the flames of justice.

A spirit of fire has anointed us, too, for a great task— and the Holy Spirit sustains us through hope. When the apostles first received the Holy Ghost in the *Book of Acts,* the Spirit anointed them through flaming tongues. Before the Spirit came upon them, the disciples were powerless to perform the work Christ had commanded for them. Having been ignited by the gift of the Holy Spirit, the disciples went forth to do God's work in the world. Like Katniss, we must be set aflame before we can begin our work in the world—in our case, the work that the Gospel has set before us.

Like Katniss, we must be set
aflame before we can begin our
work in the world—in our case,
the work that the Gospel has set
before us.

Reading 10
All Life is Precious to God

Matthew 25:40 (NRSV) *"Truly I tell you, just as you did it to one of the least of these who are members of my family, you did it to me."*

DURING THE 74ᵀᴴ Hunger Games, Katniss forms an alliance with Rue, the female tribute from District 11. Rue is the youngest contestant and is therefore particularly vulnerable; despite her resourcefulness and speed, she is considered an easy target. Her strengths as a survivor are overlooked by most of the tributes, who believe that she is too small and weak to pose a real danger. Yet Katniss discovers there is more to Rue than meets the eye. After Rue helps Katniss escape from the pack of Careers, Katniss and Rue form a friendship, and work together to stay alive. The alliance does not last long. Rue is captured and brutally murdered before Katniss's eyes.

In the entire trilogy of *The Hunger Games*, only one moment resembles religious ritual—Rue's funeral. Overcome with grief, Katniss defies the Capitol's disregard for human life by taking a moment during the games to honor Rue. She gathers flowers, sings a song, and says good-bye to the innocent child who has fallen victim to the Capitol's twisted Games. In this quiet, simple, and yet profound moment, Katniss forces the viewers (and us) to pause and remember that Rue is not merely a face, an expendable character, but a real and whole person. She reminds us that all life is precious.

As Christians, we affirm the dignity of all human beings, and we have a responsibility to uphold the value of human life. To God, all life is precious. We are his children, and he loves us all equally. Perhaps the oldest and most widely accepted axiom in the world is, "Do unto others as you would have done unto you." The Bible itself affirms that because we are made in the image of God, we have a duty to treat everyone with respect and dignity.

As Christians, we affirm the dignity of all human beings, and we have a responsibility to uphold the value of human life

Reading 11
Be True to Yourself and to God

Romans 12:2 (NRSV) *"Do not be conformed to this world, but be transformed by the renewing of your minds."*

A S A COMMENTARY on the shallowness of any voyeuristic culture, Collins frequently dwells on appearances. For example, she devotes many lengthy passages describing costuming and fashion; whether a dress designed by Cinna or a debate about hairstyles, Katniss's outer facade is continually manipulated to project a particular image. The author also gives the activities of media an unusually high level of prominence throughout the story, and her characters frequently reflect on the role of cameras, media propos, interviews, and public broadcasts. The reapings, the Caesar Flickerman interviews, the televised Games, Beetee's hacked television propos—all of these play an extremely important role in the unfolding of the narrative of the *Hunger Games*. Collins also carefully demonstrates how rigidly controlled and contrived so much of these surface-level appearances actually are: the media is used for propaganda on all sides, and Katniss clearly knows her appearance is being engineered for various purposes.

Against the barrage of shallowness and falsehoods that seem true on the surface, Collins crafts the character of Peeta as a figure extremely concerned with truth. One night before their first Hunger Games, Peeta and Katniss have an important conversation on the roof of their temporary home in the Capitol, during which he tells Katniss: "I don't want them to change me in there. Turn me into some kind of monster that I'm not." Surrounded by stylists and cameras, Peeta nonetheless remains true to his pure self; this is shown especially by his steadfast and unchanging love for Katniss. Even when the Capitol hijacks him, Peeta's primary concern is to regain his ability to discern the truth (as evidenced by his perpetual refrain of "Real or not real?"). Peeta never willingly compromises who he is in order to please someone else—in fact, he is the very image of genuine truth and reality, a character who refuses to conform to the patterns of his world.

God calls us to live virtuously and deeply. Christ tells his followers to seek the truth in all things. When we have difficulty discerning what is real and not real, we only have to ask God to guide us. However, when we become caught up in appearances, we can lose ourselves to the things that simply do not matter. We can be in the world, but it is important that we do not become molded to it. When we submit ourselves to Christ, we let go of the things that tie us to this world—and in doing so, we gain so much more: truth, depth, wholeness, and perfection.

God calls us to live virtuously and deeply

Reading 12
Choose Your Friends Wisely

Proverbs 1:10 & 16 (NASB) *"My child, if sinners entice you, do not consent . . . for their feet run to evil, and they hurry to shed blood."*

GOING INTO THE Hunger Games competition, Katniss knows that one of the common strategies—especially among the Careers—is for some tributes to band together and kill others until only those in their own alliance remain. During the 74th Hunger Games, Cato, Glimmer, Marvel, and Clove form an alliance with a few others; Katniss even suspects Peeta to be part of this alliance for a time before he saves her life. Katniss herself forms an alliance first with Rue and then later with Peeta. But throughout most of *The Hunger Games*, she feels uneasy about the concept of alliances altogether. Knowing that eventually she must kill those with whom she forms a bond, these partnerships seem a dangerous mental game. In fact, she does become so attached to Peeta by the end of the competition that she risks both of their lives with the poisoned berries rather than break the alliance.

Peeta and Katniss survive their first Hunger Games largely because they have wisely chosen to stick together no matter what comes their way (including Seneca Crane's announcement at the end that one of them must kill the other). In the Quarter Quell, they again find themselves part of an alliance; this time, it is much larger and comprised of an unexpected group of tributes. Those who band together around Peeta and Katniss protect the District 12 tributes and save both of them from harm, often risking their own lives. Mags runs into the fog so Peeta can escape; Finnick revives Peeta when he is knocked unconscious; and Johanna removes Katniss's tracker, leaving herself vulnerable enough to be picked up by the Capitol. The other alliance formed during the Quarter Quell—comprised of Brutus, Enobaria, Cashmere, and Gloss—is contrastingly depicted as bloodthirsty, ruthless, and ultimately loyal to none but their own selves.

The Bible warns us to choose our friends wisely. Jesus tells his disciples that they did not choose him, but he chose them so that they could "bear fruit that will last." Elsewhere, he says, "A good tree cannot bear bad fruit, nor can a bad tree bear good fruit." We can test whether our friendships are healthy and holy by asking ourselves what kind of fruit they bear. If our friendships cause us to behave cruelly, mercilessly, or greedily, we must reexamine our choices. However, when our friendships encourage us to live with greater love, grace, and kindness toward our neighbor, we can be sure that we are forming alliances that are pleasing to God.

We can test whether our friendships are healthy and holy by asking ourselves what kind of fruit they bear

Reading 13
At Whose Expense…?

Ezekiel 16:49 (ESV) *"This was the guilt of your sister Sodom: she and her daughters had pride, excess of food, and prosperous ease, but did not aid the poor and needy."*

IN THE HUNGER *Games* trilogy, the Capitol is depicted as the height of excess, greed, and selfishness. Even before Katniss arrives in the Capitol for her first Hunger Games, she is overwhelmed by the excess of food, drink, and staff employed on the train to the city. While she has often gone for weeks without proper meals, Katniss suddenly finds herself in the Capitol surrounded by sumptuous buffets—seemingly inexhaustible amounts of food. Though her family had to fight for everything, the people of the Capitol are waited on hand-and-foot by servants, usually an avox: someone whose tongue has been removed in punishment for rebellious acts. The people of the Capitol are extremely vain, spending inconceivable amounts of money to alter their appearances or stock up on the latest fashion trends. Her experience in the Capitol is so starkly contrasted to life in District 12 that Katniss is utterly repulsed by it; indeed, as Plutarch Heavensbee later confirms in *Mockingjay*, the purpose of the districts is to provide the Capitol its "bread and circuses."

Nothing symbolizes the grotesque excess of the Capitol's regime as well as the drink offered to Peeta during their victory tour. In *Catching Fire*, when Katniss and Peeta stop in the Capitol during their victory tour of Panem, a lavish banquet is thrown in their honor. Even Katniss is taken in by the rich delicacies presented to them that evening. However, at one point Flavius offers an oversatiated Peeta a drink that will make him vomit so he can continue to eat. The incident not only destroys both Katniss and Peeta's appetites, but it also reminds them of the Capitol's stop-at-nothing attitude toward satisfying the desires of its selfish inhabitants.

Given to pride, greed, and excess, the Capitol in Collins's series closely resembles the city of Sodom in the Bible. The people of Sodom were overrun by their lust and greed; they profited by exploiting the poor and the vulnerable. Christ commanded us to care for the poor, to tend the sick, and to visit those in prison. Yet so often Christians become caught up in the luxuries of life that they fail to follow God's command to live simply and care for the poor. At whose expense do you receive your bread and circuses?

Christ commanded us to
care for the poor, to tend the sick,
and to visit those in prison. Yet so
often Christians become caught up
in the luxuries of life that they fail
to follow God's command to live
simply and care for the poor

Reading 14
Christ is the Bread of Life

Matthew 26:26 (NRSV) *"While they were eating, Jesus took a loaf of bread, and after blessing it he broke it, gave it to the disciples, and said, 'Take, eat; this is my body.'"*

L ET'S THINK ABOUT bread for a moment: Collins uses bread throughout the *Hunger Games* trilogy as a symbol of life and hope and generosity. The name "Panem" literally means "bread," and since bread symbolizes the most basic food necessary for survival, it is an apt name for the nation. Bread becomes an important part of Katniss's experience in the Hunger Games. During the 74th Hunger Games, she receives a loaf of life-sustaining bread when she is on the verge of starvation; and in the Quarter Quell, twenty-four loaves are sent to the allied tributes, providing both sustenance and a message about how to escape to safety.

Peeta comes from a family of bakers, and he himself has a talent for baking. Katniss therefore closely associates bread with Peeta—"the boy with the bread" who saved her life long before they ever came to the arena. Once, when food was particularly scarce for Katniss and her family, Peeta saw her on the street, malnourished and near starvation. To save her life, Peeta gave Katniss a loaf of burned bread. This gesture of kindness cost Peeta, as his mother punished him with a beating after she discovered what he had done. For this reason, Peeta's gift of the bread stays with Katniss for the remainder of her childhood, and throughout the series she continually refers to him as "the boy with the bread."

Jesus is often called the "bread of life" because the bread he gives us is life giving and feeds our very spirit. He tells his disciples that bread alone cannot sustain human life; we need the gift of God's Word to live wholly, deeply, and fully. Thus, God gives us his Son to be the living bread on which we can feed our souls. Before Christ died on the cross, he held a dinner for his friends in which he told him that his own body was to become bread, and his blood, wine. When Peeta gives Katniss the bread, he extends life-giving sustenance; yet even with this bread, Katniss will one day be subject to death. God gives us his only Son to be our everlasting bread so that we can live forever. To live our lives fully and faithfully, we need only rely on the bread that God gives to us in Christ.

Jesus is often called the "bread of life" because the bread he gives us is life giving and feeds our very spirit.

Reading 15
God Judges the Heart

1 Samuel 16:7 (NCV) *"People look at the outside of a person: but the LORD looks at the heart."*

ONE OF THE many disturbing aspects of the Hunger Games is that sponsors choose to whom they will send gifts based on appearance and odds. Katniss knows that she is being judged on her looks from the moment she enters the Capitol; to gain favor with the citizens of Panem, she must present herself in a sympathetic way while also demonstrating her potential as a contender. Her clothes, mannerisms, words, actions—everything is put under severe scrutiny, not just by the game makers, but by all of Panem. Furthermore, people gamble on the odds of the children selected for the Hunger Games based on the appearance of the tributes. Rue does not have favorable odds because she is young and vulnerable, but tributes such as Cato have very good chances; even these kinds of factors effect whether or not the tributes will receive gifts in the arena.

We are all guilty of judging others based on their

appearances. As fallen human beings, we often count unimportant things as important: we value money, possessions, attractive bodies. Very often we consider a person's worth to be tied to these external things. God does not see the same way people see. While we look at the outside and judge a person's worth based on what is immediately apparent, God looks into our hearts. Kindness, graciousness, a love for justice—these are the things God finds valuable. We can rejoice that God does not judge us on our appearance or our chances of success in our earthly lives. Instead, we know that God sees deep into our hearts and knows the content of our soul; thus, instead of trying to prove our worth through an outward appearance, we are called to develop the content of our character from within.

God does not see the same way people see. While we look at the outside and judge a person's worth based on what is immediately apparent, God looks into our hearts.

Reading 16
God Chooses Love before Justice

James 2:13 (NRSV) *"For judgment will be without mercy to anyone who has shown no mercy; mercy triumphs over judgment."*

THROUGHOUT THE *Hunger Games,* Katniss Everdeen feels torn between two men whom she loves dearly and whose characters represent different essential virtues. On the one hand, she loves Gale Hawthorne, her hunting partner and confidant with whom she has developed an intimate friendship over many years. Gale is impassioned by a hunger for justice and a desire to free Panem's poor and oppressed people from their suffering. Katniss admires his passion for justice, but while she certainly has feelings for Gale, she knows they are not as strong as his feelings for her.

Katniss also loves Peeta Mellark, to whom she forms a deep attachment through their experience of the Hunger Games. By contrast to Gale, Peeta embodies the virtue of unwavering, unconditional love—love that goes on loving even when its object fails to reciprocate, love that forgives many times over. Katniss's love for Peeta develops over time, and throughout the entire series she fails to dedicate herself to Peeta with the same commitment and certainty with which he dedicates himself to her; yet despite her lack of commitment, Peeta never stops loving Katniss.

Throughout most of the *Hunger Games* trilogy, Katniss feels torn between her love for Gale and her love for Peeta. Yet in the end, she realizes that she always needed Peeta's unwavering and forgiving love more than she needed Gale's passion for justice. Only love can rescue her from her own shortcomings.

God desires both justice and mercy, and he wants us to live our lives by these two virtues. He tells us to seek the welfare of others, to stand up for the oppressed and to take up the cause of those who are enslaved. He passionately desires us to live and love in freedom. However, our desire for freedom and justice should follow the example of Christ: in his redemptive act on the cross, he frees us through love. God dictates justice by the law of Love. Because God loved us, he earnestly desired for us to live free from the bonds of sin. Yet in his love, he did not condemn us but sent his son to be the sacrifice of love to make us free. Yes, we are called to work for justice in the world—but that work should always be fueled by love.

God dictates justice by the law of Love. Because God loved us, he earnestly desired for us to live free from the bonds of sin. Yet in his love, he did not condemn us but sent his son to be the sacrifice of love to make us free.

Reading 17
Our Eyes on Jesus

Job 42:2 (NRSV) *"I know that you can do all things, and that no purpose of yours can be thwarted."*

A T THE END of *Mockingjay*, Katniss sees her sister among a group of rebel medical aides brought to the Capitol to help the victims of a brutal attack. As soon as the medical team reaches the victims, a bomb explodes and kills everyone, including Prim. This moment is the most devastating experience for Katniss in the entire trilogy. All of her efforts have been driven by a desire to protect her sister from harm. The story begins when she volunteers for the Games to save her sister, so it seems an unbearably cruel twist that Katniss loses Prim in the final moments of the war. In the wake of this devastating loss, Katniss struggles to comprehend what her purpose has been, and only after time has passed can she remember that her cause has become something much larger.

Sometimes we might work very hard toward a noble goal, just to have our efforts foiled at the last minute. In these moments, it can be easy to lose hope; we might even be tempted to ask God why he allowed our good intentions to fail. The disciples themselves experienced this kind of devastation in the hours after Christ's death. Believing that their leader was gone forever, they despaired that they had followed a path leading to a dead end. For a moment, they lost sight of the bigger picture: they could not trust that God had a plan for them. When Jesus appeared to them after the Resurrection, they were overjoyed; their faith was renewed, and their vision for God's plan restored.

Even when we feel that our hard work leads nowhere or that our good intentions are unrewarded in the end, we trust that God has a plan. God works out his purposes in mysterious ways. Even when it seems like our work has been for nothing, we just need to keep our eyes on Jesus, and he will use our lives for his perfect purposes.

Even when it seems like
our work has been for nothing, we
just need to keep our eyes on Jesus,
and he will use our lives for his
perfect purposes.

Reading 18
God Does Not Fearmonger

Matthew 12:7 (NRSV) *"But if you had known what this means, 'I desire mercy and not sacrifice,' you would not have condemned the guiltless."*

I**N ADDITION TO** sending children to be sacrificed at the Hunger Games, the citizens of Panem are cruelly expected to celebrate the games and express gratitude to the Capitol as well as repentance for past rebellions. At the reaping, the mayor of District 12 tells the audience that the Hunger Games are a time for "thanks and repentance." The implication here is that the Games were designed to call those who rebelled against the Capitol to repent for their insurrection, and that they should be "grateful" that the Capitol showed "mercy" by not simply slaughtering every remaining man, woman, and child. In truth, these calls to gratitude and contrition are thinly veiled scare tactics and propaganda. Thus, since the mayor's words are so contrived, they inspire fear, terror, and anger rather than repentance and thanks.

Genuine repentance cannot be born out of

terrorizing. For this reason, God does not fearmonger in his dealings with us. Though we constantly fail to love God and our neighbor as we should, God does not hold a grudge against us. Nor does he demand sacrifices to show how sorry we are for our sins. No, instead he asks that we have a "contrite heart," meaning that we acknowledge ourselves as sinful creatures and we genuinely try to be better and live in Godly love. God cares nothing for an outward show; he prefers instead a sincere heart and a will to change for the better. Further, Christ commands us to follow God's example by forgiving those who offend us. He commands us to be merciful, just as our Father in Heaven is merciful.

God cares nothing for an outward show; he prefers instead a sincere heart and a will to change for the better.

Reading 19
We Are All Responsible for
Tikkun Olam

Jeremiah 29:7 (NRSV) *"But seek the welfare
of the city where I have sent you into exile,
and pray to the Lord on its behalf, for in its
welfare you will find your welfare."*

O N THE MORNING before the reaping, Gale
proposes to Katniss that they escape into the
woods to safety. He tells her that they have the
skills to survive alone in the woods, away from the
district and all of its injustices. From the tone of the
conversation, it is apparent that this is not the first
time Gale has suggested such a plan. Katniss feels
very uncomfortable even discussing the idea because
she has Prim and her mother to look after, and Gale
himself has a large family for whom he provides
food. While Gale admits that there are too many lives
depending on both himself and Katniss for survival,
he also holds onto his idea to leave District 12. In
Catching Fire, he agrees to Katniss's desperate plan
to take all their family and run away, but he refuses
to accommodate Peeta. Only when Gale is prepared

to take all of District 12 with him can he make his escape, but this is no flight from duty to others. On the other hand, Gale's decision to lead the District 12 refugees to District 13 involves great risks and willingness to take responsibility.

Sometimes we may want to run away from our responsibilities to make the world a better place, but as Christians we know this is not an option. Jewish theology teaches a fundamental concept called *tikkun olam*, which means "the healing of the world"—essentially, tikkun olam maintains that we all have a responsibility to work toward making this world a better place. This concept therefore upholds our responsibility to *this world*, as the Kingdom of God is attainable on earth. And indeed, while God promises to renew the earth, he also commands us to participate in the renewing work. Each of us is responsible to contribute to the righting of injustices, the conservation of the earth, and the sharing of God's good news with our brothers and sisters in this mortal existence. Only by fulfilling our duty to heal our world can we participate in God's great and redemptive plan for us.

Sometimes we may want to
run away from our responsibilities
to make the world a better place,
but as Christians we know this is
not an option.

Reading 20
The Only Thing We Owe is
Allegiance to God

Psalm 103:10 (NRSV) *"He does not deal
with us according to our sins, nor repay us
according to our iniquities."*

DURING THEIR FIRST Hunger Games, Katniss
tells Peeta that she so vividly remembers the
time he gave her bread because she does not like
to owe people. Because Peeta saved her life in their
youth, she feels indebted to him on principle. In
his kindness, Peeta continues to protect Katniss
during their lead-up to the Games and during the
Games themselves. However, Katniss resents his help
because, in her mind, she now owes Peeta in return
for his generosity and protection. Throughout the
trilogy, Katniss shows an extreme aversion to the
idea of "owing" others for their actions. She worries
that she will always owe Haymitch for bringing her
and Peeta out of the Games alive; she feels that she
owes Finnick after he saves Peeta during the Quarter
Quell; and she understands Thresh's feeling that he
"owes" her for trying to protect Rue. While Katniss

also expresses appropriate gratitude to both District 11 and the Hob for sending gifts to her during the Hunger Games, her overall preoccupation with owing others demonstrates that she fears being unable to "make even" the score of kindnesses that are shown to her.

Thank goodness this is not how God wants us to understand generosity or kindness! We do not live by an economy of love, always trying to balance the scales and make even one deed for another. We are called simply to live generously. God does not deal with us according to what we owe, because if he did, we would never be worthy to worship him. Instead he offers us his Son Jesus as a final and eternal "payment" of all our debts. Yet in sacrificing his Son for us, God does away with the economic approach to love, because by giving something so perfect in exchange for something so imperfect, God destroys the balances altogether. Thanks to this sacrifice of his Son, all that we owe to God is our love, honor, and praise.

We do not live by an economy
of love, always trying to balance
the scales and make even one deed
for another. We are called simply
to live generously

Reading 21
Christ Gives Us Courage

John 16:33 (NRSV) *"I have said this to you, so that in me you may have peace. In the world you face persecution. But take courage; I have conquered the world!"*

I N CATCHING FIRE, Katniss goes into the woods one day to visit a secret cabin she believes to be abandoned. When she arrives, she discovers that two refugees from District 8 named Bonnie and Twill have taken shelter in the cabin. Although at first the two women fear that Katniss means to harm them, once they recognize her, they welcome her and share what they know about the uprising in District 8. The situation Twill relays can only be described as horrific: after the rebels initially but briefly secured the main buildings, the Capitol sent enough Peacekeepers to District 8 to obliterate the rebel strongholds and enforce a district-wide lockdown. Now the district is run by peacekeepers. It is overrun with starvation, and the main source of income for District 8's people—the uniform factory—has been bombed, killing everyone inside.

Bonnie and Twill barely escaped District 8 with their lives. They stole peacekeeper uniforms, escaped on a train to District 6, and then continued on foot all the way to District 12. Having nothing left to lose and facing persecution and hunger, the two women banned together and risked everything they had. Twill tells Katniss that their final destination is District 13, which as far as they know may not even exist. In fact, the Capitol has always maintained that it was completely destroyed during the first Uprising. Therefore, Bonnie and Twill have chanced everything to make a journey based entirely on hope and remote possibility. Their desperate circumstances have given these women an unusual degree of courage to seek something better.

Sometimes extreme circumstances call us to act with great bravery—and indeed, God desires us to live lives courageously and to persevere. Christ warned his followers that we will face persecution. Though he was afraid, he himself willingly suffered the persecution of the cross. While we can have confidence in Christ's promise of eternal life and salvation, our faith does not call us to live without risks, and we are never promised safety in this present life. Yet when we look to the example of Christ, we know that we can overcome our fear to work toward the greater Good. Just as he put his faith in God's greater plan, so too may we trust that God rewards our bold faith by fulfilling his promise to redeem us in the end.

Yet when we look to the example of Christ, we know that we can overcome our fear to work toward the greater Good.

Reading 22
God Loves a Generous Heart

Mark 12:43–44 (ESV) *"He said, 'Truly I tell you, this poor widow has put in more than all of them; for all of them have contributed out of their abundance, but she out of her poverty has put in all she had to live on.'"*

DURING HER FIRST trip to the Hunger Games, Katniss receives a loaf of bread from the citizens of District 11. She knows that they have sent it to her in gratitude for the tender way she honored Rue's death in the arena, and she immediately marvels at what it would have cost the impoverished people of District 11 to send such a generous gift. She has learned from Rue about the horrific conditions in District 11—especially the widespread hunger and starvation—so she knows that this loaf of bread represents the height of generosity and the willingness of District 11's citizens to think of her needs before their own. She thinks to herself, "How many would have had to scrape up a coin to put in the collection box for this one loaf?"

This reflexive question might bring to mind a story from Matthew's Gospel with which many Christians are familiar. One day in the temple, Christ directs his disciples' attention to a poor widow who places two coins in the collection box. Though these two coins amount to a mere penny, Christ tells his disciples that her gift to the Temple is more generous than the gifts of the rich; while the rich may contribute more capital than the poor widow, she gives from an abundance of her heart. Like the generous citizens of District 11, and like the poor widow in Matthew's Gospel, we are directed by Christ to cultivate generosity in our own hearts. God does not desire wealth, but genuine action and the will to give of ourselves out of our poverty.

We are directed by Christ to cultivate generosity in our own hearts

Reading 23
Honesty Reaps Rewards, but Falsehood Brings Consequences

Proverbs 12:19 (NRSV) *"Truthful lips endure forever, but a lying tongue lasts only a moment."*

IN A WORLD fueled by lies and deception, it is no wonder that the Hunger Games are rife with deceit. Many tributes will present themselves as weak only to later ambush the others with unforeseen strength. Tributes will form alliances only to break them at the critical moment—even Peeta participates in such a deception. However, perhaps the cruelest and most consequential deception in all of the *Hunger Games* occurs in the unfolding romance narrative of the first novel. To win sponsors, Katniss knows that she must convince viewers that she and Peeta are madly in love, and she allows herself to become caught up in this enormous lie. Unfortunately, Peeta is not lying, and he is devastated at the end of the competition when he realizes that Katniss has been using him to survive. Katniss's insincere declaration of love truly spins out of control in *Catching Fire*, when President Snow commands her to convince all of Panem—especially Snow himself—that she truly does love Peeta. When she fails, it puts both of their lives at stake.

In *Mockingjay*, Peeta is hijacked by the Capitol and can no longer distinguish between truth and fiction. His hostility and anger toward Katniss is understandable: although he certainly has been brainwashed, Peeta nonetheless knows that Katniss has never been entirely honest with him about her love. She continually wavers between loving Peeta and wanting to be with Gale. She has been lukewarm in her love for Peeta at the best of times, and Peeta's memories of Katniss thus dwell on her most deceitful moments. Katniss wants to blame Haymitch, Plutarch, Finnick, and the others whose secret plan resulted in Peeta's capture. She feels she has been wrongfully deceived, that she should have been informed about the plan. But although a little honesty from the rebels may have helped Peeta, it is almost certain that if Katniss had been straightforward with him, he would not have ended up so vulnerable to the Capitol's unusual methods of torture.

Throughout the New Testament, sin is equated with deceit, and for this reason Christ tells his followers that the "truth will set you free." When we speak truthfully and live our lives according to sincerity, we live in the truth and we are free from the consequences of deceit. But when we lie, whether to God, others, or ourselves, we cannot live in truth. God is not so concerned with the small lies we tell one another as with the lies we tell ourselves: the lie that we can manage without God's help, or that we love God and our neighbor as we should. It can be very difficult to admit to ourselves the truth of our own shortcomings and weaknesses—especially the ways in which we fall short of loving others— but this is what God demands of his followers. When we are honest with ourselves before God, we embark on the journey to healing and freedom that is promised in Christ Jesus.

It can be very difficult to
admit to ourselves the truth
of our own shortcomings and
weaknesses—especially the ways
in which we fall short of loving
others— but this is what God
demands of his followers.

Reading 24
Hope Comes in Small Packages

2 Corinthians 3:12 (NRSV) *"Since, then, we have such a hope, we act with great boldness."*

WHY DO THE rebels in the districts persevere in their fight against the Capitol, despite the overwhelming odds against them? The poor and the oppressed across Panem refuse to give up, despite their lack of power or resources. What gives them their hope?

Throughout the *Hunger Games* series, hope comes to those who need it in unlikely packages: a gift of bread sent from one of the poorest districts; a well-designed dress that gives Katniss a competitive edge; a Mockingjay baked into a piece of bread as a symbol of the rebellion. These seemingly small things come at the right moment and help the heroes of the *Hunger Games* survive the trial they are facing.

Nothing gives those in the districts so much hope as their victors. They are "the embodiment of hope where there is no hope." The victors of the Hunger Games so aptly symbolize hope because, having overcome the Games, they defy the absolute power of the Capitol—they show the Capitol that some in the districts are still strong enough to survive against incredible odds. Therefore, to the people of Panem, the victors are the source of hope when hope seems impossible, and no one embodies such hope as much as Katniss Everdeen, who not only survived the Games but brought her fellow District 12 tribute out alive with her. She thus defies all the rules of the Capitol and proves that the citizens of Panem might be craftier and stronger than the Capitol believes.

As Christians, how do we understand hope? The writer of the Epistle to the Hebrews says that "faith is being sure of what we hope for and certain of what we do not see." Paul, in his letter to the Corinthians, identifies hope as one of the three great theological virtues (the others are faith and love). And the psalmist writes many times over that our hope is in God.

Against the odds, the citizens of Panem continue to believe that something good could happen for them—by placing their faith in Katniss and the rebellion, they hold onto the hope that life will be better. This is not unlike the Christian understanding of hope. For indeed, when we place our hope in Jesus, we are saying "Though I do not know what the outcome of my circumstances may be, I trust that God will make things right." When we hope in the power of the resurrection, we center our expectations and our confidence in the knowledge that God loves us and that this love is enough to conquer death itself.

When we hope in the power
of the resurrection, we center our
expectations and our confidence
in the knowledge that God loves
us and that this love is enough to
conquer death itself.

Reading 25
God Promises to Sustain Us Forever

1 Corinthians 15:58 *"Therefore, my beloved, be steadfast, immovable, always excelling in the work of the Lord, because you know that in the Lord your labor is not in vain."*

After Katniss shoots the arrow that kills Coin at the end of *Mockingjay*, she sinks into despair. Her moment has come and gone: after Prim died, her one wish was to kill Snow personally, and in the end she chose to point her arrow elsewhere. While she does not regret her decision, Katniss believes she now no longer has any reason to go on living. She spends days in the hospital trying to die—hoping she will bleed to death, looking for a window to jump from, and even trying to starve herself. The worst part of her suffering is her knowledge that she has lived out her usefulness as the Mockingjay for Panem's rebels—a feeling exacerbated by the loss of her sister, and the knowledge that even Prim mattered nothing to those who used her for their own gain. When Plutarch meets her after her trial has finished, he even tells

Katniss that no one knows what to do with her now that the war is over, although if another comes up, he is sure they could find a role for her.

For Christians, using people in this way is unacceptable. Thank goodness God does not cast us aside once we have lived out our usefulness! Again, God does not operate in an economy of love, judging us according to what we can offer him or how much we accomplish. He certainly cares that we dedicate our lives to a worthy cause—the cause of love—but even when our time here on earth does come to an end, it is only a beginning. When God uses us, we do not feel drained and emptied; instead, God replenishes our supply over and over when we allow ourselves to be vessels of his love. As long as we know that we have run the race with faith and perseverance, we can know that God will see us through to eternal life and joy in his Kingdom of Love.

When God uses us, we do not feel drained and emptied; instead, God replenishes our supply over and over when we allow ourselves to be vessels of his love.

Reading 26
The Danger of Distraction

1 Peter 5:8 (NRSV) *"Discipline yourselves; keep alert. Like a roaring lion your adversary the devil prowls around, looking for someone to devour."*

IN CATCHING FIRE, President Snow visits Katniss in the Victor's Village with a warning: during the course of her victory tour, she must convince all of Panem—and especially Snow—that her love for Peeta is sincere. Snow tells Katniss that the districts are becoming unruly because she has sparked rebellion in the people of Panem. If she fails to prove that her trick with the berries was motivated by love and not rebellion against the Capitol, everyone she loves will suffer. Snow's order shakes Katniss so much that she spends the whole tour completely focused on proving her love for Peeta to all of Panem. When the tour is finished and Katniss meets with Snow again, he tells her that she has not succeeded in her task.

Several weeks later, Katniss finds herself at a cabin in the woods talking to refugees Bonnie and Twill. She learns that the districts have been ripe for rebellion for a long time, that her actions could never have "derailed the moment building in District 8." She realizes that President Snow used her and Peeta to distract all of Panem from their plans to rebel. Peeta and Katniss's public performances of love and adoration, their engagement, their plans for the wedding—all of this has been designed by Snow to distract the rebels. And, in allowing herself to become wrapped up in Snow's threats against her friends and family, Katniss, too, has been distracted.

One of Jesus's most common exhortations to his disciples is to "be vigilant." He warns his followers to be alert, for they do not know the hour when the Son of Man will return. He tells the parables about being prepared—the bridesmaids with their lamps and the thief in the night. And when he goes to Gethsemane to pray on the night of his betrayal, Christ asks his friends to "stay awake and watch" for just one hour with him. Clearly, Jesus was warning his followers to be wary of the things that distract from our true calling! It can be very easy to become distracted by the things of this world, but Jesus warns us to stay vigilant to God's plan and purpose. What things distract you from being true to God's calling in your life? If you know that something is causing you to stray from the path that God has laid before you, how might you free yourself from that distraction?

Clearly, Jesus was warning his followers to be wary of the things that distract from our true calling!

Reading 27
Exercise Gratitude

1 Thessalonians 5:18 (NRSV) *"give thanks in all circumstances; for this is the will of God in Christ Jesus for you."*

ONE OF THE most touching moments in the trilogy occurs in *Catching Fire* when Peeta promises part of his earnings as a victor to the families of Thresh and Rue. While Katniss is initially paralyzed by guilt and fails to offer proper thanks for the gift of bread she received from District 11, Peeta instinctively offers what she considers "the perfect gift." He announces his intent to give the money after a lengthy speech about how both Rue and Thresh saved Katniss—and thereby saved Peeta—from death. He notes that he and Katniss will be unable to ever repay the debt, but as a token of thanksgiving for the gifts given by the District 11 tributes to the District 12 victors, he pledges one month's earnings to the families of the dead tributes. He therefore makes this sacrificial and generous gesture in an outpouring of gratitude, knowing that without Rue and Thresh, he and Katniss would not have emerged victorious from the arena.

"Thanks be to God, who gives us the victory through our Lord Jesus Christ!" So writes Paul in his second letter to the Corinthians. One of the best ways we can honor Christ in our lives is to live in gratitude to him. Through Jesus's sacrifice, God has given us victory over death. It is our duty to remember the promise of salvation at all times and never cease thanking God for this gift. We have done nothing to deserve the love that God gives to us, and yet he never stops loving us. He even carries that love all the way to the cross, through death, and finally into the new life promised by his resurrection. Thanks be to God!

Through Jesus's sacrifice,
God has given us victory over
death. It is our duty to remember
the promise of salvation at all times
and never cease thanking
God for this gift

Reading 28
Forgive Always, Everyone, an Infinite Number of Times

Luke 6:37 (NRSV) *"Forgive, and you will be forgiven."*

A S READERS OF the *Hunger Games* series, we should find it difficult to observe how Katniss treats Peeta. Because Katniss holds those for whom she cares at an arm's length, never allowing herself to become too close, she inflicts deep wounds upon others. Of all the people who Katniss fails to love properly, Peeta bears the deepest scars. Despite the fact that he commits himself unconditionally to loving Katniss, she refuses to commit herself wholly to him. She continues to keep a foot in the door with both Peeta and Gale as potential lifelong mates, and in doing so, she keeps the attention of both men *at their expense*. Indeed, Katniss makes neither Gale nor Peeta happy; yet while Gale seems as though he may find love elsewhere, Peeta clearly states that he will only ever love Katniss. Her lack of faithfulness, therefore, cuts him to pieces.

However, Peeta never holds a grudge for very long. After their first Hunger Games together, he is angry that Katniss used him to survive, but he does not stay mad very long, and when he comes around, he even apologizes for having been angry with her. While he feels hurt about the way events unfold in *Catching Fire*—even to the point of being unable to enjoy their engagement—he nonetheless forgives Katniss and continues to love her. Even in *Mockingjay*, as he works to regain his memory by reliving all the moments when Katniss has hurt him, he eventually forgives her for her faithlessness and again commits himself to helping her recover. The only reason Katniss and Peeta find love together in the end is because Peeta willingly forgives Katniss for the many times she has been disloyal, lukewarm, or even cruel.

When Peter asked Jesus how many times we ought to forgive others, Jesus told him that we must forgive "seventy times seven" times. It can be easy for us to start doing math—70x7=490, so we forgive 490 times—but this is not what Jesus asks of us. The number itself is insignificant. Jesus, in fact, commands us to forgive everyone always. If God, who is faultless, can forgive us for our many faults against him, why should we be unable to forgive others for their transgressions against us? The best way to help us live lives of forgiveness and reconciliation is to always remember that each of us has sinned and fallen short of God's glory. If we remember this, we will be reminded that God has been gracious to us, and therefore we must be gracious to others.

Jesus, in fact, commands us to forgive everyone always. If God, who is faultless, can forgive us for our many faults against him, why should we be unable to forgive others for their transgressions against us?

Reading 29
We Are What We Watch

Ephesians 5:11 (NRSV) *"Take no part in the unfruitful works of darkness, but instead expose them."*

ONE OF COLLINS'S greatest achievements in the *Hunger Games* trilogy is that she so adeptly forces us into a reflexive reading practice. To read a story reflexively means that we must interpret our participation as readers as part of the meaning of the story itself. Because Collins's trilogy so powerfully indicts a voyeuristic culture—a culture that enjoys watching blood sport so much that it becomes wrapped up in the so-called "glamour" of the Games— we must consider our own place as onlookers into this story. She writes in such a compelling manner that we cannot help being entertained. And what does this say about us as a culture, that we are able to suspend belief and indulge in brutally violent stories for the sake of our entertainment? Are we really that different from the citizens of Panem who, in watching children murder one another, become complicit in these horrific crimes?

Indeed, it is not a crime to read novels such as *The Hunger Games*—unless we are unwilling or unable to recognize our own participation in the violence these stories depict. Unless we allow the *Hunger Games* to speak to us about the curse of sin in our lives, we will fail to find a Christian message. As Christians, we are called to be "children of the Light." Once we were in the darkness of sin, but because of Christ, we are now able to walk in the Light. This does not mean that we are free from sin, but rather that we must be willing to acknowledge and recognize sin order that we may flee from it.

Does the *Hunger Games* affirm the virtues of love, sacrifice, forgiveness, and generosity? Of course. Yet if we read the story reflexively, we experience a much deeper Christian response than an affirmation of these virtues. We are invited to acknowledge our part in human suffering; and in recognizing ourselves as sinners, we are further invited to turn from sin to God. When we read stories such as these, we are given the opportunity to ask ourselves: Am I truly living as God wishes me to live?

We are invited to acknowledge
our part in human suffering; and
in recognizing ourselves as sinners,
we are further invited to turn
from sin to God.

Reading 30
Turn to Christ

Ezekiel 33:11 (NRSV) *"Say to them, As I live, says the Lord God, I have no pleasure in the death of the wicked, but that the wicked turn from their ways and live; turn back, turn back from your evil ways; for why will you die, O house of Israel?"*

SUZANNE COLLINS SETS her story in a dystopian nation of the future that seems far from the world as we know it today. It is hard to imagine our civilization declining to the degree depicted in the *Hunger Games* trilogy. Will we really backslide so far? Surely Collins's story is just that: a story. Fiction. Set in the future and far from reality.

Yet any discerning reader will know that this is simply not true. The novels are as much a powerful warning to the present as a piece of fiction set in the future. Though Collins does not give us a detailed account of Panem's history, she does tell her readers that the nation "rose up from the ashes of a place that was once called North America." The people who inhabited this land used up the earth's resources, suffered under severe climate change, and waged devastating wars against each other over what little land remained. Given the reality of climate change, human greed for the earth's resources, and mankind's propensity to inflict violence on his fellows, it is not actually all that difficult to imagine such a chain of events.

God does not desire that anyone should be lost to sin and death. Throughout the Bible, he calls us to repent of our sins and return to him. Though we may neglect to live faithfully in our relationship with God, he is never unfaithful to us; if only we turn unto him, we are promised freedom and new life through God's Son. All of us will stray from God at one time or another in our lives; yet if we do not stray too far, we will find many signposts directing us back to the way we should go.

Fiction can serve as a powerful signpost. Collins's *Hunger Games* trilogy is effective as a tool for Christian reflection because it serves as a stern warning about our need for God and a powerful reminder that we must repent of our human error and return to him. In fact, as Christians, we should readily understand that the world described in the *Hunger Games* serves as a completely realistic conception of what the earth would look like if we did entirely forsake God. If we utterly rebel against God, our planet will become a hostile outpost of human misery and sin, perhaps a world not unlike Panem. Indeed, if we forget the God who gives us life and love and health, is it so difficult to imagine our world becoming like the one depicted in the *Hunger Games*? When we read this story, Collins invites us (whether knowingly or unknowingly) to repent of our own errors and return to the God who loves us—the God who always remembers and is faithful to his promise.

Though we may neglect to
live faithfully in our relationship
with God, he is never unfaithful to
us; if only we turn unto him, we are
promised freedom and new
life through God's Son

Also by Selena Sarns

50 Shades of Black and White:
A Biblical Response to 50 Shades of Grey

The Gospel According to Les Miserables:
30 Devotions to Inspire Faith

About the publisher
TheBiblePeople.com exists to help people read,
understand, and apply the Bible.

Follow us on Facebook:
Facebook.com/TheBiblePeople